Phonics Fun

Songs, rhymes and stories by Jean Bunton

1

Contents

Unit	Letter(s)	Sound	Page
1	p	/ p /	1
2	b	/ b /	3
3	c/k	/ k /	5
4	g	/ g /	7
Review 1			9
5	t	/ t /	11
6	d	/ d /	13
7	s	/ s /	15
8	z	/ z /	17
Review 2			19
9	m	/ m /	21
10	n	/ n /	23
11	l	/ l /	25
12	r	/ r /	27
Review 3			29
13	f	/ f /	31
14	v	/ v /	33
15	h	/ h /	35
16	w	/ w /	37
Review 4			39
Phonics Dictionary			41

Listen to these words.

1

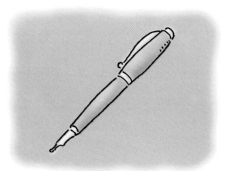

pen

2

pet

3

pig

4

put

5

panda

6

pencil

Sing the song.

Panda in the park,
Panda in the park,
Having so much fun
Like the panda in the park.

 **ACTIVITY** Draw the panda in the park on your own paper.

Listen to these words.

1

bag

2

bed

3

big

4

bike

5

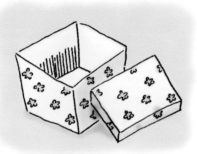

box

6

bus

Say the rhyme.

One thing I like
Is my big blue bike.
I keep it in a box
With my little blue socks.

**What is in your bag?
Show and tell.**

I like my ...

4

c/k

Listen to these words.

1

cat

2

cup

3

cake

4

key

5

king

6

kite

Say the rhyme.

One little cat
With one little key
Can drive a car.

One little king
With one little kite
Can fly to a star.

Say the rhyme in pairs.

Listen to these words.

1
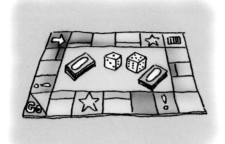
game

2

go

3

give

4

get

5

good

6

gun

Sing the song.

Go and get a game,
Get a game to play.
Give it to your sister,
And have a good day.

Who do you want to play with?
Sing the song again.

Give it to Mary ...

Say the words.

1

pen
Ben

2

pig
big

3

pin
trash **b**in

4

cat
get

5

car
girl

6

kite
give

7

come
game

8

bed
pet

9

cup
put

Choose and write nine words. Play bingo.

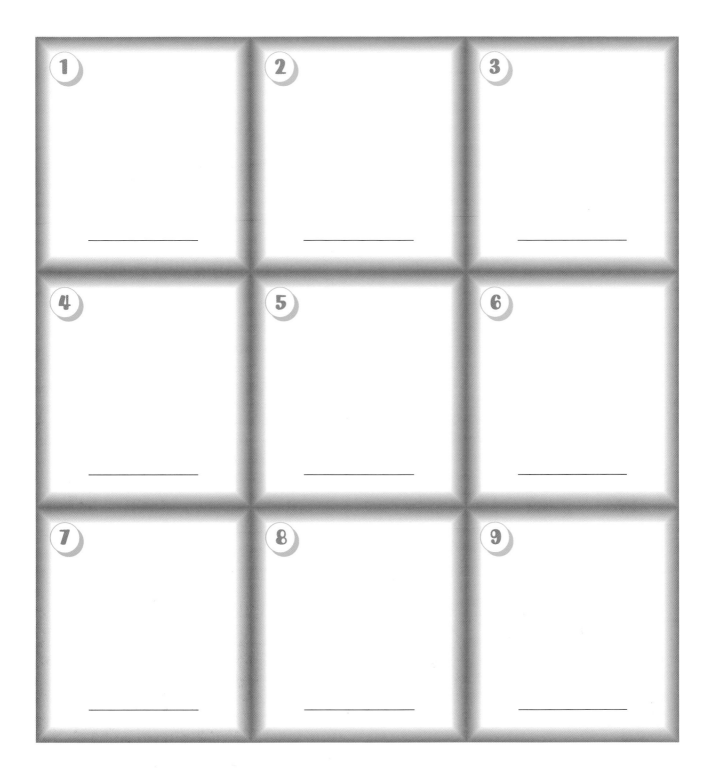

Listen to these words.

1

tap

2

tell

3

ten

4

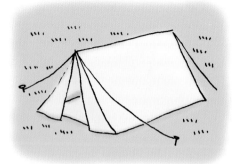

tent

5

taxi

6

tiger

Sing the song.

Ten tall boys standing in a tent.
The tent falls down,
The tent falls down.

Ten tall boys sleeping in a tent.
Ten tall boys,
No more noise.

 **Act the song.**

Listen to these words.

1

Dad

2

desk

3

dog

4

door

5

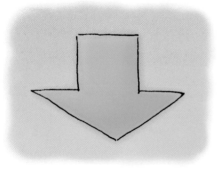

down

6

duck

Say the rhyme.

The dog and the duck
Get into the car.
Dad drives them home.
How happy they are.

ACTIVITY Act the animals and Dad in the car.
Say who you are.

duck ... duck

Dad ... Dad ...

14

Listen to these words.

1

sad

2

see

3

sick

4

sit

5

sun

6

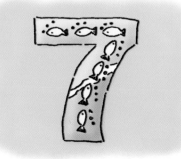

seven

Say the rhyme.

We all sit down,
We all sit down,
As fast as we can,
We all sit down.

We all stand up,
We all stand up,
As fast as we can,
We all stand up.

 Act the rhyme.

Listen to these words.

1

zipper

2

zoo

3

zebra

4

do**z**en

5

la**z**y

6

pu**zz**le

Say the rhyme.

A dozen zebras in the zoo
Start to think what they should do.

A dozen ice creams on a plate,
Eat them now or it's too late.

 Act the rhyme.

Play the game. Say the words.
Draw the route.

Listen to these words.

1

man

2

me

3

Miss

4

moon

5

monkey

6

Mommy

Sing the song.

I can see a monkey,
Standing on the moon.
Clap his hands,
Clap his hands,
There's a monkey on the moon.

Who else is on the moon? Sing the song again.

Listen to these words.

1

nap

2

neck

3

net

4

noon

5

not

6

nut

Read the story.

I take a nap.

I dream of noodles!

I catch fish in my net.

I eat nuts all afternoon.

 **Act the story.**

Listen to these words.

1

lamp

2

leg

3

lock

4

love

5

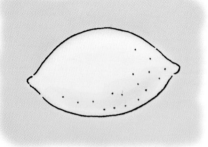

lemon

6

lucky

Sing the song.

Look at me!
I'm as lucky, as lucky as can be.
Look at me!
I'm as lucky, as lucky as can be.
Happy as a clown, busy as a bee,
Look at me, look at me!

Listen to these words.

1

rat

2

red

3

run

4

rabbit

5

ruler

6

rock

Sing the song.

Jump   up   and

                   down

Like a red rubber ball,
Jump up and down
Like a red rubber ball,
Jump up and down like me!

 **Act the song.**

28

Play the game in pairs. Say the words.

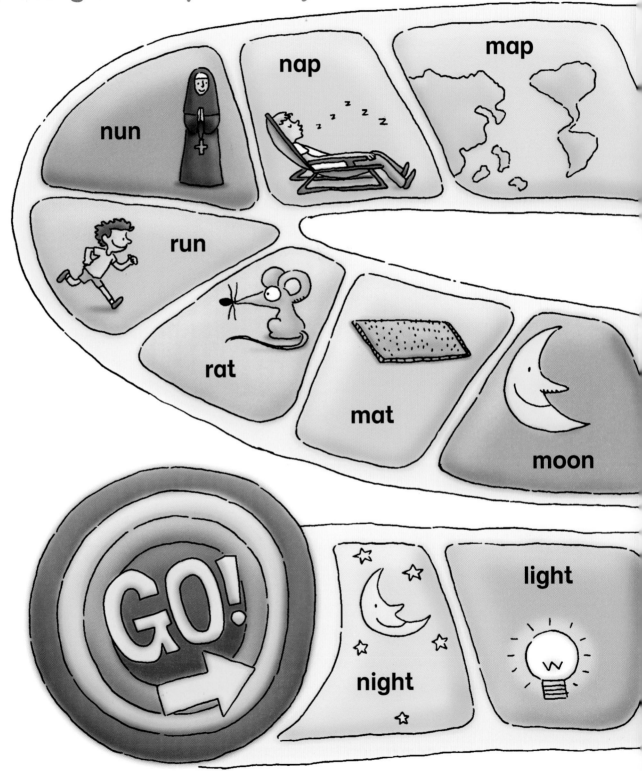

Miss

Mommy

YOU WIN!

noon

9 nine

line

right

rock

lock

lamp

Listen to these words.

1

fan

2

fat

3

fish

4

fox

5

ferry

6

funny

Say the rhyme.

I can swim like a fish,
A very funny fish,
I can swim like a very funny fish.

I can run like a fox,
A very furry fox,
I can run like a very furry fox.

 **Act the fish and the fox.**

Listen to these words.

1

van

2

vet

3

visit

4

fi**v**e

5

gi**v**e

6

lo**v**e

Read the story.

The vet looks after dogs and cats.

He visits horses, pigs and cows.

He makes them feel very good.

They all love the vet.

 **Think of other animals that the vet visits.**

Listen to these words.

1

hat

2

he

3

hit

4

hot

5

happy

6

hippo

35

Sing the song.

Come and see the hippo
Sleeping in the mud.
Sing a happy hippo song.

With a hat on his head,
And mud for his bed.
Sing a happy hippo song.

 **Say "happy hippo" as fast as you can.**

36

Listen to these words.

1

wall

2

week

3

wet

4

win

5

window

6

woman

Say the rhyme.

It's wet, it's wet,
It's very, very wet,
It's wet and windy today.
It's wet, it's wet,
It's very, very wet,
Too wet to go out and play.

 **Do you like wet and windy weather? Ask and say.**

Play the game. Say and write the words.

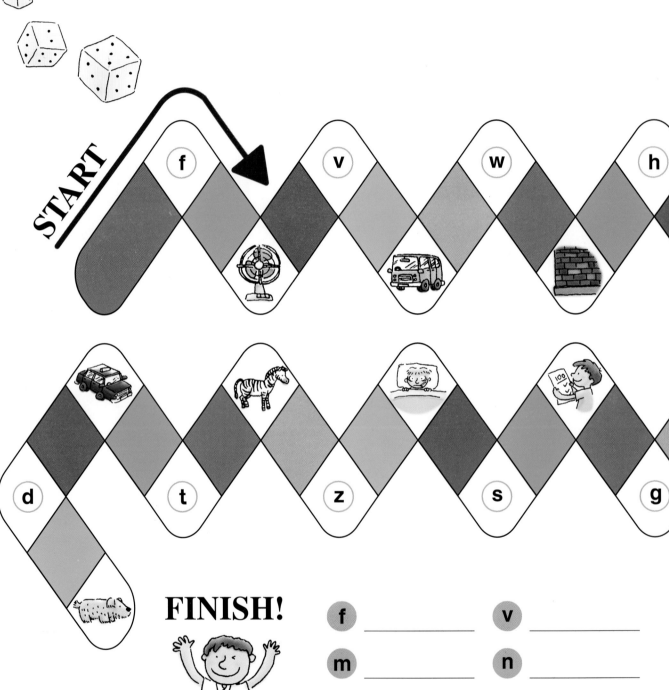

START

f v w h

d t z s g

FINISH!

f _____ v _____

m _____ n _____

g _____ s _____

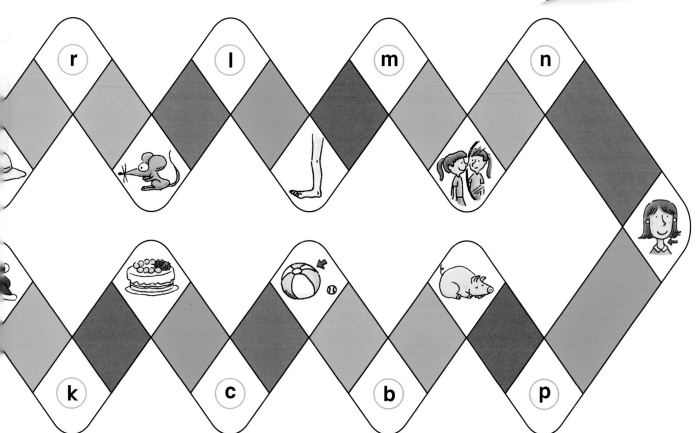

r   l   m   n

k   c   b   p

w _____   h _____   r _____   l _____

p _____   b _____   c _____   k _____

z _____   t _____   d _____

Phonics

p pen   pet   pig   put panda pencil

b bag bed big   bike box bus

c/k cat cup cake key   king kite

g game go give get good gun

41

Dictionary

t

tap	tell	ten	tent	taxi	tiger

d

Dad	desk	dog	door	down	duck

s

sad	see	sick	sit	sun	seven

z

zipper	zoo	zebra	dozen	lazy	puzzle

Phonics

m   **m**an   **m**e   **M**iss   **m**oon   **m**onkey   **M**ommy

n   **n**ap   **n**eck   **n**et   **n**oon   **n**ot   **n**ut

l   **l**amp   **l**eg   **l**ock   **l**ove   **l**emon   **l**ucky

r   **r**at   **r**ed   **r**un   **r**abbit   **r**uler   **r**ock

Dictionary

f

fan	fat	fish	fox	ferry	funny

v

van	vet	visit	five	give	love

h

hat	he	hit	hot	happy	hippo

w

wall	week	wet	win	window	woman

Published by
Pearson Longman Asia ELT
20/F Cornwall House
Taikoo Place
979 King's Road
Quarry Bay
Hong Kong

fax: +852 2856 9578
email: pearsonlongman.hk@pearson.com
www.pearsonlongman.com

and Associated Companies throughout the world.

First published 2002

This American English Edition first published 2004
Reprinted 2012 (twice)

Produced by Pearson Education Asia Limited, Hong Kong
SWTC/28

ISBN-13: 978-962-00-5459-4
ISBN-10: 962-00-5459-8

Worksheets

1

A Say the words. Circle the letter p in the words.

1

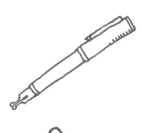

pen

2

put

3

panda

4

pencil

B Listen and write the missing letters.

The panda has a ___en and a pencil.

Now say the sentence and color the picture.

Date: _____

A What sound do they begin with? Write the beginning letters.

1

☐

3

☐

2
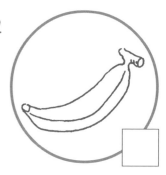
☐

4

☐

5
☐

B Listen and circle the letters **p** or **b**.

1
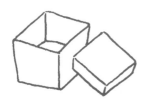
| p |
| b | ox

2

| p |
| b | ed

3

| b |
| p | en

4

| b |
| p | anda

Now say the words.

A Say the sentences. Circle the letters c or k.

1 The cat has a kite.

2 The kid has a car.

B Write the words in the crosswords. Then say the words.

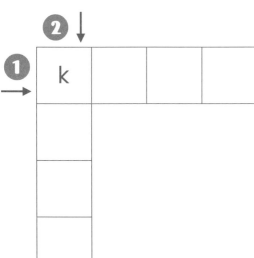

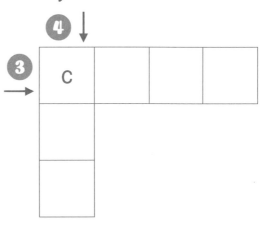

1

2

3

4

Date: _____

A Circle the words that begin with the letter **g**. Write the words next to the correct pictures.

g	a	m	e
k	g	e	t
g	i	v	e
p	g	o	c

1 _____

2 _____

3 _____

4 _____

B Listen and circle the correct beginning letters.

1

g c k

2

g c k

3

g c k

4

g c k

Date: _____

A Listen and write the missing letters.

1

Ben has a __en.

2

The __ig is __ig.

3

The __irl has a __ite.

B Join the words with the same beginning sounds.

(p)   (b)   (c / k)   (g)

Date: _____

A Write and say the words.

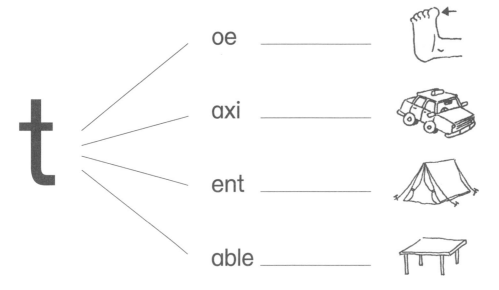

t

oe _____

axi _____

ent _____

able _____

B Listen and write the missing letters.

Tom's __ail is in the __ea.

Now say the sentence and color the picture.

A Listen and write the missing letters.

1 _og   **2** _esk   **3** _oor   **4** _octor

Now write the numbers next to the correct pictures.

B Listen and circle the correct letters.

1 The [d/t] uck talks to the [d/t] iger.

2 The [d/t] urtle is named [D/T] aisy.

Date: _____

 A Listen and write the missing letters. Write the numbers next to the correct pictures.

1 __it

2 __wim

3 __ing

4 __leep

B Write and say the words. Color the pictures of the words with the **s** sound.

1

_____

2

_____

3
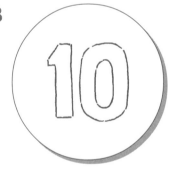
_____

4

_____

5

_____

6

_____

A Listen and write the missing letters. Circle the things in the picture.

1  _ipper

2  _ebra

3  pu_ _le

B Listen and write the letters **s** or **z**.

1 la_y

2 _ick

3 _un

4 _oo

A Listen and circle the correct words.

1 The **duck / tub** is in the tent.

2 The sad **zebra / sister** sits in the sun.

B Write the missing letters. Say the words.

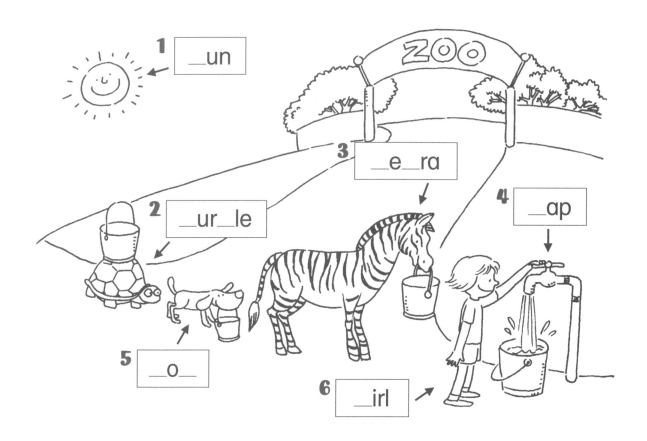

1 __un

3 __e__ra

4 __ap

2 __ur__le

5 __o__

6 __irl

A Write the words in the crossword. Then say the words.

B Listen and write the missing letters. Read the story.

There's a __an on the __oon. There's a __onkey on the __oon. The __an eats a __ango. The __onkey says "Hi" to __e.

n

Date: _____

A Write the missing letters. Practice with your own names.

My __ame's Nancy.
What's your __ame?

My __ame's John.

B Listen to the words. What letters do they begin with? Write the letters
m or **n**.

1

n

2

3

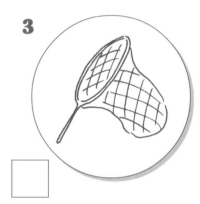

4

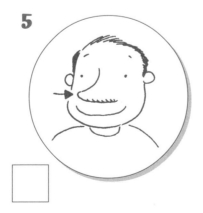

5

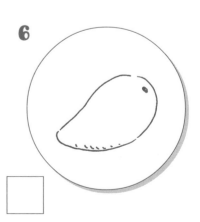

6

A Write the missing letters. Say the words.

1 _emon

2 _amp

3 _unch

4 _eaf

B Listen and finish the sentences.

1 Lucy has long _egs.

2 There is a _amp.

3 I _ove my _aby brother.

4 The _ey is in the _ock.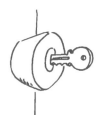

 A Listen and write the missing letters.

1 __at   **2** __abbit   **3** __obot   **4** __uler

Now write the numbers next to the correct pictures.

  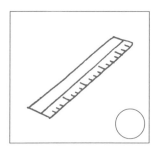 

 B Listen and write the missing letters. Say the sentences.

1 Look! There's a __abbit on the __oad.

2 Look! There's a __at on the __uler.

Review 3  Date: _____

 A Listen and circle the correct words.

1  Lucy turns on the **light / right**.

2  Rob has a **lot / not** of sweets.

3 The **moon / noon** is on the **right / night**.

B What are they? Write the words in the correct places.

m _____ _____	n _____ _____
r _____ _____	l _____ _____

Date: _____

A Circle the things beginning with the letter **f**. Write the words.

1 _ _ _

2 _ _ _ _

3 _ _ _ _

4 _ _ _ _ _

B Listen and write the missing letters.

1    The _ _x is on the _ _rry.

2    The _ _sh has a _ _ower.

3    The _ _x is _ _t.

Date: _____

A Circle the words with the letter **v**. Fill in the missing letters.

v__ __

__ __v__

v__ __

5

__ __v__

m	w	v	e	t
v	i	s	i	t
l	o	v	e	e
v	a	n	n	v
o	f	i	v	e

B Write and say the words. Color the pictures of the words with the **v** sound.

1

_____

2

_____

3

_____

4

_____

h

Date: _____

 A Listen and write the missing letters.

1 _air   **2** _at   **3** _ippo   **4** _it   **5** _ome

Now write the numbers under the correct pictures.

_____   _____   _____   _____   _____

 B Listen and circle the correct words. Read.

Harry is **hot / dot / not**.

He has a lot of **fair / hair / home**.

He is wearing a **bat / hat / cat**.

A Listen and circle the correct words.

1 　　　The **wall / ball** is tall.

2 　　　The woman is **wet / tall**.

3 　　　**Willy / Billy** plays with Winnie.

B Listen and write the missing letters.

Nancy __alks with Mary.

She has a __at.

Write the words beginning with the letters **h** or **w** in the correct boxes.

h

w

A Listen and write the missing letters.

f   v   h   w

1 _an   **2** _an

3 _at   **4** _all

5 _et   **6** _et

B Listen and write the missing letters.

1 The _oman, the _ippo and the _ox are in the _an.

2 Vera has a _lower in her _air.

Published by
Pearson Longman Asia ELT
20/F Cornwall House
Taikoo Place
979 King's Road
Quarry Bay
Hong Kong

fax: +852 2856 9578
email: pearsonlongman.hk@pearson.com
www.pearsonlongman.com

and Associated Companies throughout the world.

© Pearson Education Asia Limited 2004

First published 2002

This American English Edition first published 2004
Reprinted 2012 (twice)

Produced by Pearson Education Asia Limited, Hong Kong
SWTC/28

ISBN-13: 978-962-00-5459-4
ISBN-10: 962-00-5459-8

Worksheets

1

Name: _____

Class: _____

PEARSON
Longman

pearsonlongman.com

ISBN 978-962-00-5459-4

9 789620 054594